Have Yourself a
Punny Little Christmas

DD683919

Also by Richard Lederer

Adventures of a Verbivore
Anguished English
Basic Verbal Skills (with Phillip Burnham)
The Bride of Anguished English
The Circus of Words
Comma Sense (with John Shore)
Crazy English
The Cunning Linguist
Fractured English
The Giant Book of Animal Jokes (with James Ertner)
Get Thee to a Punnery
Literary Trivia (with Michael Gilleland)
A Man of My Words
The Miracle of Language
More Anguished English
The Play of Words
Pun & Games
Puns Spooken Here
The Revenge of Anguished English
Sleeping Dogs Don't Lay (with Richard Dowis)
The Word Circus
Word Play Crosswords, vols 1 and 2 (with Gayle Dean)
Word Wizard
The Write Way (with Richard Dowis)

Have Yourself a Punny Little Christmas

WORD PLAY FOR

THE HOLIDAYS

Richard Lederer

Illustrations by
Jim McLean

Wyrick & Company

CHARLESTON

First Edition
09 08 07 06   10 9 8 7 6 5 4 3 2 1

Published by
Wyrick & Company
An imprint of Gibbs Smith, Publisher
P.O. Box 667
Layton, UT 84041

Orders: 1.800.748.5439
www.gibbs-smith.com

Designed by Mary Ellen Thompson, TTA Design
Printed and bound in the United States of America

Library of Congress Cataloging-in-Publication
Data

Lederer, Richard, 1938-
   Have yourself a punny Christmas / Richard
Lederer ; illustrations by Jim McLean.—1st ed.
     p. cm.
   ISBN 0-941711-80-3
   1. Christmas–Humor. 2. Puns and punning. I. Title.

PN6231.C36L43 2006
818'.602–dc22

                                          2006007702

To the Walk Family Trust,
for its great generosity

Contents

�

1

The True Meanings of Christmas

The great English etymologist Owen Barfield once wrote that "words may be made to disgorge the past that is bottled up inside of them, as coal and wine when we kindle or drink them yield up their bottled sunshine." When we uncap the sunshine that is stored inside the many words that relate to the Christmas season, we discover that the light that streams forth illuminates centuries of human history and customs.

The word *Christmas* derives from the Old English *Cristes maesse*, meaning "the festival mass of Christ." *Christmas* is a fine example of a disguised compound—a word formed from two independent morphemes (meaning-bearing elements) that have become so closely welded together that their individual identities have been lost.

Christmas is the only annual religious holiday to have received official and secular sanction by all the states. The word *holiday* itself is another disguised compound, descending from the Old English *haligdaeg*, "holy day." With the change in pronunciation has come a change in meaning so that holidays, such as Independence Day and Labor Day, are not necessarily holy. The *day* morpheme in *holiday* has also transmogrified so that one (especially if one is British) can go "on holiday" for more than one day.

In English-speaking countries, the day following Christmas Day is called Boxing Day. This expression comes from the custom which started in the Middle Ages around 800 years ago: Churches would open their alms boxes, in which people had placed gifts of money, and distribute the contents to poor people in the neighborhood on the day after Christmas. The tradition continues today; small gifts are often given to couriers such as postal staff and children who deliver newspapers.

The name *Christ* is a translation of the Hebrew word messiah, "the anointed one," rendered through the Greek as *Khristos*. Jesus also reaches back to ancient Hebrew and the name Yeshua (Joshua), which is explained as "Jah (or Jahveh, i.e. Jehovah) is salvation."

We learn about Jesus through the *gospels*. *Gospel* is yet another disguised compound, from the Old English *god*, "good," and *spel*, "news." The four gospels spread the good news of the life and work of Christ. No surprise then that the four men who wrote the gospels are called *evangelists*, from the Greek *euaggelion*, which also means "good news."

The babe was born in *Bethlehem*, a Hebrew word variously interpreted as meaning "house of bread or food," "house of fighting," or "house of the god Lahamut." The Christ child was laid in a *manger*, a word related to the French verb *manger*, "to eat." Why? Because Jesus's crib was a large wooden box that had served as a trough for feeding cattle.

We call the worship of the new-born babe the *Adoration*, from the Latin adoratio: *ad-* "to," *oro-* "pray"; hence, "to pray to." Among those who came to worship were "wise men ... from the East," *magi*, a Latin word for "magician." Magi were members of an ancient Persian priestly caste of magicians and sorcer-

ers. Incidentally, the number of wise men is never specifically mentioned in the gospels; we infer three from the gifts bestowed on the Christ child.

The letter X is the first letter of the word *Xristos*, which in Greek is the word for Christ. *Xmas*, then, is actually a Greek derivative that does not eradicate the name of Christ from *Christmas*. But in reality it is really a legitimate term that is used within the Greek Orthodox church.

Yuletide as a synonym for the Christmas season dates back to a pagan and then Christian period of feasting about the time of the winter solstice, December 22. The origin of *yule* is uncertain. One suggestion is that *yule* comes from the Gothic *giul*; or *hiul*, which meant "wheel." In this context, *yule* signifies that the sun, like a wheel, has completed its annual revolution. The Gothic *ol* or *oel* and the Anglo Saxon *geol*, all meaning "feast," and the Middle English *yollen*, "to cry aloud," have also been considered as sources for *yule*.

Whence the *tide* in *Yuletide*? From an Old English word meaning "time," as in *Eastertide* and "Time and tide wait for no man."

Among the most fascinating Christmas etymologies are those for *Santa Claus* and *Kriss Kringle.* When the Dutch came to the New World, the figure of St. Nicholas, their patron saint, was on the first ship. After the Dutch lost control of New Amsterdam to the English in the seventeenth century, *Sinterklaas* (a form of St. Nikolaas) gradually became anglicized into *Santa Claus* and acquired some of the features of the English Father Christmas.

Father Christmas is based on a real person, St. Nicholas. Nicholas was a Christian leader from Myra (in modern-day Turkey) in the 4th century A.D. He was shy and wanted to give money to poor people anonymously. It is said that one day he climbed the roof of a house and dropped a purse of money down the chimney. It landed in a stocking that a girl had put to dry by the fire. This explains the belief that Father Christmas comes down the chimney and places gifts in children's stockings.

Kriss Kringle reflects an even more drastic change from one language to another. The Germans and German-speaking Swiss who settled in Pennsylvania in the early eighteenth century held the custom that the Christ Child, "the Christkindl," brought gifts for the children on Christmas Eve. When these Pennsylvania German (also known as Pennsylvania Dutch) communities were joined by English-speaking settlers, the Christkindl became *Kriss Kringle.* By the 1840s, Kriss Kringle had irretrievably taken on the identity of St. Nicholas, or Santa Claus. Slogans like "Put the Christ back in Christmas" were coined in an effort to remind people of the holiday's origin.

The word *carol* came from a Greek dance called a choraulein, which was accompanied by flute music. The dance later spread throughout Europe and became especially popular with the French, who replaced the flute music with singing. People originally performed carols on several occasions during the year. By the 1600s, carols involved singing only, and Christmas had become the main holiday for these songs.

Most of the carols sung today were originally composed in the 1700s and 1800s. They include "O Little Town of Bethlehem" and "Hark! The Herald Angels Sing." The words of the famous carol "Silent Night" were written

on Christmas Eve in 1818 by Joseph Mohr, an Austrian priest. Franz Gruber, the organist of Mohr's church, composed the music that same night, and the carol was sung at midnight Mass. "O Holy Night" was introduced at midnight Mass in 1847. Adolphe Adam, a French composer, wrote the music. Popular nonreligious carols include "Jingle Bells" and "White Christmas."

Of the various plants associated with the Christmas season, the poinsettia possesses the most intriguing history etymologically. A Mexican legend tells of a penniless boy who presented to the Christ Child a beautiful plant with scarlet leaves that resembled the Star of Bethlehem. The Mexicans named the plant *Flor de la Noche Buena*, "Flower of the Holy Night," for Dr. Joel Roberts Poinsett, the first U.S. minister to Mexico, discovered the Christmas flower there in 1828 and brought it to this country, where it was named in his honor in 1836. The poinsettia has become one of the most popular of Christmas plants—and one of the most misspelled and mispronounced *(pointsettia, pointsetta, poinsetta)* words in the English language.

Another botanical Christmas item is the pear tree. In the seasonal song "The Twelve Days of Christmas," have you ever wondered why the true love sends not only a partridge but an entire pear tree? That's because in the early French version of the song the suitor proffered only a partridge, which in French is rendered as *une pertriz*. A 1718 English version combined the two—"a partridge, une pertriz"—which, slightly corrupted, came out sounding like "a partridge in a pear tree." Through a process known as folk etymology, the partridge has remained proudly perched in a pear tree *(une pertriz)* ever since.

A Merry Christ Mass
and Happy Holy Days to all!

✿

11
A Stockingful of Christmas Puns

✖

How do cats greet each other at Christmas?
"Have a Furry Merry Christmas and a Happy Mew Year!"

How do sheep greet each other at Christmas?
"Season's Bleetings and Fleece Navidad! Fleece on earth, good wool to men!"

Punnery is largely the trick of compacting two or more ideas within a single word or expression. Punnery challenges us to apply the greatest pressure per square syllable of language. Punnery surprises us by flouting the law of nature that pretends that two things cannot occupy the same space at the same time. Punnery is an exercise of the mind at being concise. Punnery is a rewording experience, especially around Christmas time. That's when people exchange hellos and good buys with each other, the time of year when every girl wants her past forgotten and her presents remembered, the time of year when mothers have to separate the men from the toys.

———————————

When does Christmas come before Thanksgiving?
In the dictionary.

If athletes get athlete's foot, what do astronauts get?
Missile toe.

What do you call a Christmas bird dog?
A point setter.

What do you say to a bad puppy at Christmas?
"Felix, naughty dog!"

What disasters could happen if you dropped the Christmas turkey?
The downfall of Turkey, the breakup of China, and the otherthrow of Greece.

What do you call a manufacturer of
turkey filling?
A stuffing stocker.

Why is a Christmas turkey
a fashionable bird?
*Because he always appears
well dressed for dinner.*

What do you call a bunch of parents
standing in line to buy their daughters a
popular doll?
A Barbie queue.

What do elves learn in school?
The elf-abet.

What's the best thing to put into a
Christmas cake?
Your teeth.

What do you call an ephant and
a cam at Christmas?
No "el," no "el."

Why are Christmas trees like
bad knitters?
They both drop their needles.

What do movie stars burn in their
fireplaces at Christmas time?
Holly wood.

What do you get when you cross a
gift-wrapper with a wise guy?
Ribbon Hood

What do you call elephants at Christmas?
Noelephants.

What did the classical musician use to
keep track of what he wanted to buy for
Christmas?
A Christmas Chopin Liszt.

What did Jack Frost say to
Frosty the Snowman?
"Have an ice day!"

What do you call a chicken in
the North Pole?
Lost.

What do Frosty and his snowgirlfriend
ride to get around in the winter?
An icicle built for two.

Where do they live?
Lake Snowbegone.

What do snowmen eat for breakfast?
Frosty Flakes.

What do snowmen eat for lunch?
Icebergers and frozen brrrgers.

What do you call a snowman
who's a thief?
An ice burglar.

Where do snowmen go to dance?
Snow balls.

Where do snowmen keep their money?
In a snow bank.

Why did Frosty decide to live in
the middle of the ocean?
Because snowman is an island.

What do you get when you cross a snowman with Dracula?
Frostbite.

What do you get when you cross Santa
Claus with a tramp?
A ho-ho-bobo.

Who hides in the bakery at Christmas?
A mince spy.

Have you heard about the neurotic doll
that's so popular this Christmas?
It's wound up already.

Have you heard that they're planning to combine Chanukah and Christmas? The new song for the amalgamated holiday will be *"Oy Vay, Maria."*

Did you hear about the dyslexic devil worshipper?
He sold his soul to Santa.

What do you call a ghost hanging around Santa's Workshop?
A North Pole-tergeist.

What happened to the little boy who swallowed Christmas tree trimmings?
He contracted tinselitis.

Why did the little girl say when she was invited to portray the Virgin in a Christmas pageant?
"Oh, good. Now I can eat, drink, and be Mary."

What do snowmen and snowwomen wear on their heads?
Snow caps.

Knock-knock.
Who's there?
Santa.
Santa who?
Santa package by FedEx, so it should arrive by Christmas.

Knock-knock.
Who's there?
Snow.
Snow who?
Snow business like show business.

Knock-knock.
Who's there?
Donut.
Donut who?
Donut open till Christmas.

Knock-knock.
Who's there?
Dexter.
Dexter who?
Dexter halls with boughs of holly.

Knock-knock.
Who's there?
Avery.
Avery who?
Avery merry Christmas to you!

¡¡¡
A Punderful Game

❀

That's the difference between a one-winged angel and a two-winged? Angel? *It's a matter of a pinion.*

It's a matter of my opinion that Yule love the game you're about to play. In each sentence below, fill in the blank or blanks with an expression commonly used at Christmastide or with an outrageous holiday pun. Answers repose at the end of this chapter, but don't sneak a peek until you've tried your hardest.

——————————

1. On December 24, Adam's wife was known as _____.

2. In Charles Dickens's *A Christmas Carol*, Scrooge was visited by the ghost of _____ _____.

3. An opinion survey in Alaska is called a _____.

4. What does Santa Claus do with his three gardens? _____, _____, _____!

5. What Christmas message is conveyed by these letters?:

ABCDEFGHIJKMNOPQRSTUVWXYZ
ABCDEFGHIJKMNOPQRSTUVWXYZ.

_____, _____

6. When the salt and the pepper say "Hi!" to each other, they are passing on

_____ _____.

7. A holy man bereft of change could be called _____ _____.

8. When you cross a sheep with a cicada, you get a _____ _____.

9. Actor O'Connor and actress Channing are known on December 25 as _____ _____.

10. People who tell jokes on December 25 might be called _____ _____.

11. An airplane disaster in Israel is a ____.

12. A quiet medieval armor-wearer is a

_____.

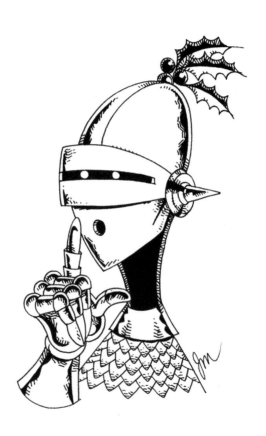

13. A cat walking on the desert is bound to get _____.

14. Who is the most famous Christmas actress?
    Halle _____.

15. What do you call it when your Christmas tree explodes? O Tannen_____

Answers

1. Christmas Eve 2. Christmas Present 3. North Poll 4. Hoe, hoe, hoe!. 5. Noel, Noel (no *l*, no *l*)

6. seasons' greetings. 7. St. Nickleless. 8. Baa! Humbug! 9. Christmas Carols 10. Christmas cards

11. cresh 12. silent knight 13. sandy claws 14. Halle Berry 15. bomb

✼

IV
A Bloopered Christmas

❀

A mother was pleased with the card her son had made her for Christmas, but was puzzled as to the scraggly-looking tree from which many presents dangled. At the very top, something that looked strangely like a bullet.

Mom asked the boy if he would explain the drawing and why the tree itself was so bare, instead of a fat pine tree. "It's not a Christmas tree," he said. "It's a cartridge in a pear tree."

"And what would you like for Christmas?" asked a department-store Santa Claus. The child stared at him open mouthed and horrified for a minute, then gasped: "Didn't you get my e-mail?"

A small boy wrote in a Christmas Card to his Aunt: "And I want to thank you for all the presents you have sent in the past, as well as all the ones you are going to send me this Christmas."

Two daughters had been given parts in a Christmas pageant at their Church. At dinner that night, they got into an argument as to who had the most important role. Finally the 10 year old said to her younger sister, "Well you just ask Mom. She'll tell you it's much harder to be a virgin than it is to be an angel."

A Sunday-school teacher was talking about Christmas and the coming of Christ and asked, "And what was the name of Jesus's mother?"

"Mary," all said.

"Now what his father's name?"

One little fellow raised his hand. "Virg."

"Virg? Where did you get that idea?"

"Well," answered the boy, "they always talk about the Virg 'n' Mary!"

A youngster drew a Christmas scene that showed Santa, sleigh, and reindeer. There were the regular eight and Rudolph plus a strange looking tenth animal. The addition looked like a cross between a reindeer and a cow with a green nose. The youngster explained that it was ... Olive, the udder reindeer.

Another Sunday-school teacher had the little ones draw pictures of the Bible stories. Little Emma proudly presented the teacher a picture of the journey to Bethlehem. The drawing showed an airplane flying over the desert. In the passenger area sat Joseph, Mary, and little Jesus.

"The drawing is fine," said the teacher, "but who's that up front flying the plane?"

Answered the girl, "That's Pontius the Pilot."

When yet another religion school teacher asked her student why there was a dog in the nativity drawing, the fledgling artist explained that it was a German shepherd.

Sunday-school boys and girls not only produce graphic misinterpretations of the Bible in their drawings; they also rewrite biblical history with amazing grace. It is astonishing what happens to the Christmas story when young scholars around the world retell it:

The King James Virgin of the Bible tells us that when Mary heard that she was the Mother of Jesus, she sang the Magna Carta and wrapped him in toddler clothes. Jesus was born because Mary had an immaculate contraption.

In the Gospel of Luke they named him Enamel. St. John, the Blacksmith, dumped water on his head. Joseph and Mary took Jesus with them to Jerusalem because they couldn't get a baby-sitter. When the three wise guys from the East Side arrived, they found Jesus laid in the manager. When Jesus grew up, he explained the Golden Rule: "Do one to others before they do one to you."

The word *mondegreen* was coined by Sylvia Wright, who wrote a *Harper's* column about the phenomenon in 1954, when she recounted hearing a Scottish folk ballad, "The Bonny Earl of Murray." She heard the lyric

Ye Highlands and Ye Lowlands
Oh where hae you been?
They hae slay the Earl of Murray,
And Lady Mondegreen.

Wright powerfully identified with Lady Mondegreen, the faithful friend of the Bonnie Earl. Lady Mondegreen died for her liege with dignity and tragedy. How romantic!

It was some years later that Sylvia Wright learned that the last two lines of the stanza were really

Ye Highlands and Ye Lowlands
Oh where hae you been?
They hae slay the Earl of Murray,
And laid him on the green.

Sylvia Wright was so distraught by the sudden disappearance of her heroine that she memorialized her with a neologism. She named such sweet slips of the ear mondegreens, and thus they have been evermore.

Children are especially prone to fresh and unconventional interpretations of the boundaries that separate words. One territory lush with mondegreens is religion. Many a youngster has recited the famous line from the 23rd Psalm as "Shirley, good Mrs. Murphy will follow me all the days of my life." Many other imaginary characters inhabit the lyrics of hymns and words from the Bible. Battalions of children have grown up singing about an ophthalmalogically-challenged ursine named Gladly—"the cross-eyed bear."

For religious mondegreens, the fracturing of Christmas carols opens up new worlds of meaning and imagination. Try singing along with these new takes on old favorites, creatively revised by children. I'm not making these up. Each is a certified, genuine, authentic Yuletide mondegreen:

* Good King Wences' car backed out
  On a piece of Stephen.

* Deck the halls with Buddy Holly.

* We three kings of porridge and tar.

* On the first day of Christmas my tulip
  gave to me.

✳ Later on we'll perspire, as we dream by the fire.

✳ He's making a list, of chicken and rice.

✳ Noel, Noel, Barney's the king of Israel.

✳ Bells on bobtail ring, Making spareribs bright.

✳ Get a yuck, get a yuck, get a yuck yuck yuck.

✳ Oh atom bomb, oh, atom bomb.

✳ On a one horse, soap, and sleigh.

✳ With the jelly toast proclaim.

✳ Olive, the other reindeer.

✳ You'll go down in Listerine.

✳ Frosty the Snowman is a ferret elf, I say.

* In the meadow we can build
  a snowman, Then pretend that he is
  sparse and brown.

* Sleep in heavenly peas, sleep in
  heavenly peas.

* Chipmunks roasting on an open fire.

* O come, froggy faithful.

* What a friend we have in cheeses.

* Where shepherds washed their socks
  by night.

* Get dressed, ye married gentlemen, get
  huffing you this May.

* You'll tell Carol, "Be a skunk, I require."

❉

V
The Night Prior to Christmas

The Reverend Clement Clarke Moore created "A Visit From Saint Nicholas" in 1823. The poem, better known as "The Night Before Christmas," from its first line, is largely responsible for the contemporary American conception of Santa Claus, including Santa's appearance, the night he visits, his method of transportation, and his bringing toys to boys and girls. It has become a tradition for parents to read this poem to their children on Christmas Eve:

'Twas the night before Christmas,
  when all through the house
Not a creature was stirring, not
  even a mouse.
The stockings were hung by the
  chimney with care,
In hopes that St Nicholas soon
  would be there.

The children were nestled all snug
in their beds,
While visions of sugar-plums
danced in their heads.
And mamma in her 'kerchief, and I
in my cap,
Had just settled our brains for a
long winter's nap.

When out on the lawn there arose
such a clatter,
I sprang from the bed to see what
was the matter.
Away to the window I flew like a
flash,
Tore open the shutters and threw
up the sash.

The moon on the breast of the new-
fallen snow
Gave the lustre of mid-day to
objects below.
When, what to my wondering eyes
should appear,
But a miniature sleigh, and eight
tiny reindeer.

With a little old driver, so lively and
quick,
I knew in a moment it must be St
Nick.
More rapid than eagles his coursers
they came,
And he whistled, and shouted, and
called them by name!

"Now Dasher! now, Dancer! now,
    Prancer and Vixen!
On, Comet! On, Cupid! on, on
    Donner and Blitzen!
To the top of the porch! to the top
    of the wall!
Now dash away! Dash away!
    Dash away all!"

As dry leaves that before the wild
    hurricane fly,
When they meet with an obstacle,
    mount to the sky.
So up to the house-top the coursers
    they flew,
With the sleigh full of toys, and St
    Nicholas too.

And then, in a twinkling, I heard on
    the roof
The prancing and pawing of each
    little hoof.
As I drew in my head, and was
    turning around,
Down the chimney St Nicholas
    came with a bound.

He was dressed all in fur, from his
head to his foot,
And his clothes were all tarnished
with ashes and soot.
A bundle of toys he had flung on
his back,
And he looked like a peddler, just
opening his pack.

His eyes-how they twinkled! his
dimples how merry!
His cheeks were like roses, his nose
like a cherry!
His droll little mouth was drawn
up like a bow,
And the beard of his chin was as
white as the snow.

The stump of a pipe he held tight in
his teeth,
And the smoke it encircled his
head like a wreath.
He had a broad face and a little
round belly,
That shook when he laughed,
like a bowlful of jelly!

He was chubby and plump, a right
    jolly old elf,
And I laughed when I saw him, in
    spite of myself!
A wink of his eye and a twist of
    his head,
Soon gave me to know I had
    nothing to dread.

He spoke not a word, but went
   straight to his work,
And filled all the stockings, then
   turned with a jerk.
And laying his finger aside of
   his nose,
And giving a nod, up the chimney
   he rose!

He sprang to his sleigh, to his team
   gave a whistle,
And away they all flew like the
   down of a thistle.
But I heard him exclaim, 'ere he
   drove out of sight,
"Happy Christmas to all, and to all
   a good-night!"

Clement Clarke Moore was best known in his day as a professor of Oriental and Greek literature at General Theological Seminary. Had he been a lawyer, "The Night Before Christmas" might have come out sounding like this:

Whereas, on or about the night prior to Christmas, there did occur at a certain improved piece of real property (hereinafter "the House") a general lack of stirring by all creatures therein, including, but not limited to a mouse.

A variety of foot apparel, e.g. stocking, socks, etc., had been affixed by and around the chimney in said House in the hope and/or belief that St. Nick a/k/a/ St. Nicholas a/k/a/ Santa Claus (hereinafter "Claus") would arrive at sometime thereafter.

The minor residents, i.e. the children of the aforementioned House, were located in their individual beds and were engaged in nocturnal hallucinations, i.e. dreams, wherein visions of confectionery treats, including, but not limited to, candies, nuts, and/or sugar plums, did dance, cavort, and otherwise appear in said dreams.

Whereupon the party of the first part (sometimes hereinafter referred to as "I"), being the joint-owner in fee simple of the House with the parts of the second part (hereinafter "Mamma"), and said Mamma had retired for a sustained period of sleep. (At such time, the parties were clad in various forms of headgear, e.g. kerchief and cap.)

Suddenly, and without prior notice or warning, there did occur upon the unim-

proved real property adjacent and appur-
tenant to said House, i.e. the lawn, a certain
disruption of unknown nature, cause, and/or
circumstance. The party of the first part did
immediately rush to a window in the House
to investigate the cause of such disturbance.

At that time, the party of the first part did
observe, with some degree of wonder and/or
disbelief, a miniature sleigh (hereinafter "the
Vehicle") being pulled and/or drawn very rap-
idly through the air by approximately eight (8)
reindeer. The driver of the Vehicle appeared to
be and in fact was, the previously referenced
Claus.

Said Claus was providing specific direc-
tion, instruction, and guidance to the approximately eight (8) reindeer and specifically identified the animal coconspirators by name:
Dasher, Dancer, Prancer, Vixen, Comet, Cupid,
Donner, and Blitzen (hereinafter "the Deer").
(Upon information and belief, it is further
asserted that an additional coconspirator
named "Rudolph" may have been involved.)

The party of the first part witnessed Claus,
the Vehicle and the Deer intentionally and
willfully trespass upon the roofs of several res-

idences located adjacent to and in the vicinity of the House, and noted that the Vehicle was heavily laden with packages, toys, and other items of unknown origin or nature. Suddenly, without prior invitation or permission, either express or implied, the Vehicle arrived at the House, and Claus entered said House via the chimney.

Said Claus was clad in a red fur suit, which was partially covered with residue from the chimney, and he carried a large sack containing a portion of the aforementioned packages, toys, and other unknown items. He was smoking what appeared to be tobacco in a small pipe in blatant violation of local ordinances and health regulations.

Claus did not speak, but immediately began to fill the stocking of the minor children, which hung adjacent to the chimney, with toys and other small gifts. (Said items did not, however, constitute "gifts" to said minor pursuant to the applicable provisions of the U.S. Tax Code.)

Upon completion of such task, Claus touched the side of his nose and flew, rose, and/or ascended up the chimney of the House

to the roof, where the Vehicle and Deer waited and/or served as "lookouts." Claus immediately departed for an unknown destination.

However, prior to the departure of the Vehicle, Deer, and Claus from said House, the party of the first part did hear Claus state and/or exclaim: "Merry Christmas to all and to all a good night!" Or words to that effect.

— Respectfully Submitted, s./ The Grinch

VI
The Abdominal Snowman

⌘

James Fenimore Cooper wrote about the life of Santa Claus. Naturally he titled it *The Deer Sleigher.* He could have also called it *The Abdominal Snowman.* On the inside cover appears a photograph of Santa taken with his North Polaroid camera.

In the pages of this exposé, you'll find out that Santa's primary language is North Polish. You'll learn that Santa and Mrs. Claus live in an icicle built for two and occasionally take a room at a ho-ho-hotel. You'll learn that Santa always wears the same suit but it stays clean because Mrs. Claus washes it in Yule Tide. You'll learn that Santa loves tending his three gardens and exulting, "Hoe, hoe, hoe!"

You'll also discover that St. Nicholas is the main Claus. His wife is a relative Claus. His children are dependent Clauses. Their Dutch uncle is a restrictive Claus. As a group, they're all renoun Clauses. And the father of Father Christmas is, of course, a Grandfather Claus.

Santa's elves are subordinate Clauses. As they make toys, they sing "Love Me Tender." That's why they're known as Santa's little Elvis. And that's why, as they put the toys in boxes and prepare them for Santa's sack, they sing wrap music.

They feel that all their strenuous efforts getting ready for Christmas are just like a day at the office. They do all the work, and the fat guy with the suit gets all the credit. And anytime he wishes, Santa can give them the sack.

A group of rebellious elves—along with their elf uncles and elf aunts—have banded together to protest the terrible conditions they've been working under. They are known as the Santanistas—and they're striving for higher elf esteem. The little fellows have decided to unionize. They call themselves the A. F. of Elves.

On Christmas Eve, Santa eats a jolly roll, leaps into his sleigh, and urges his toys to hop in the sack. Santa's sleigh always comes out

first because it starts in the Pole position. It also gets terrific mileage because it has long-distance runners on each side.

Kriss Kringle especially loves all his reindeer because every buck is deer to him. He puts bells on all his reindeer because their horns don't work. On the way to delivering gifts, he lets his coursers stop at the Deery Queen. For this they offer him their Santapplause and sing "There's Snow Place Like Home for the Holidays" and "Freezer Jolly Good Fellow!"

Santa has the right idea: Visit people just once a year, and you'll always be welcome. Of course, Santa works just one day a year—an inspiration to civil servants everywhere.

The eight reindeer love to tell jokes to Santa Clause. They always preface each joke with "This'll sleigh you!" On one night before Christmas, Santa Claus's sleigh team came up one member short because of a sudden illness. An inflatable plastic reindeer was used to fill the void in the team so no one would take notice of the missing animal. Regis, Chief of Elves, asked Santa, "Is that your vinyl Prancer?" Santa had thought about using the famous red-nose reindeer, but the the creature would never mind his manners. That's why he's called Rude-olph.

When traveling in the sleigh in inclement weather, Santa gets icicles in his beard. Real chin chillas, those. Occasionally, cosmetics fly out of the bag and into Santa's beard, causing it to known as the beard of Avon. He sometimes removes all the bells from his sleigh and travels silently through the night. One day he hopes to win a No Bell prize.

Santa is so Santa-mental that he sometimes spends all his money on the toys that he
brings to children everywhere. At those times,
he's called St. Nickeless. Children all over the
world await Santa's gifts, even the children of
ghosts, who sing to Santa, "We'll Have a Boo
Christmas Without You." After all, toys will be
toys.

Santa often guides his sleigh to Cape
Canaveral. We know this because A SANTA
AT NASA is a palindrome—a statement that
reads the same forwards and backwards.

What's red and white and black all over?
Santa Claus entering a home through a chimney. He loves sliding down chimneys because
it soots him. But he actually has a fear of getting stuck. That fear is called Santa Claus-tro-
phobia. The way to get him out of the chimney
is to pour Santa Flush on him. Occasionally
Santa falls down a chimney. Then he's Santa
Klutz. Since Santa has to go up and down a
wide variety of chimneys on Christmas,
should he have a yearly flue shot?

Whatever the obstacles, Santa always
delivers his presence in the St. Nick of time.
Then on December 26, Santa is a beat Nick.

Never forget the five ages of man:

(1) He believes in Santa Claus.

(2) He doesn't believe in Santa Claus.

(3) He dresses up to look like Santa Claus.

(4) He looks like Santa Claus.

(5) He believes he's Santa Claus.

VII
A Pun-thology of Holiday Songs

✁

A set-up pun is a conspiracy of narrative and word play. In set-up punnery, the punster contrives an imaginary situation that leads up to a climax punningly, cunningly, and stunningly based on a well-known expression or title. In a good set-up pun, we groan at the absurdity of the situation while admiring the ingenuity with which the tale reaches its foreordained conclusion.

Now it's time to be a groan-up while admiring the following narratives as they lead up to the Christmas *pun*ch lines:

Rudolph, a dedicated Russian communist and important rocket scientist, was about to launch a large satellite. His wife, a fellow scientist at the base, urged Rudolph to postpone the launch because, she asserted, a hard rain was about to fall. Their collegial disagreement soon escalated into a furious argument that Rudolph closed by shouting, *"Rudolph, the Red, knows rain, dear!"*

A man went to his dentist because he felt something wrong in his mouth. The dentist looked inside and said, "That new upper plate I put in for you six months ago is eroding. What have you been eating?"

The man replied, "All I can think of is that about four months ago my wife made some asparagus and put some stuff on it that was delicious Hollandaise sauce. I loved it so much I now put it on everything – meat, toast, fish, vegetables, everything!"

"Well," said the dentist, "that's probably the problem. Hollandaise sauce is made with lots of lemon juice, which is highly corrosive. It's

eaten away your upper plate. I'll make you a new plate, and this time use chrome."

"Why chrome?" asked the patient.

"It's simple," replied the dentist. "Dental researchers have concluded that *there's no plate like chrome for the Hollandaise!*"

———

A group of chess-playing fanatics would gather each morning in the hotel lobby to brag about their greatest victories. It seemed that each player had only triumphs and awesome feats of skill to his credit. Came a day when the hotel manager barred the group from the lobby - because he couldn't stand to hear a bunch of *chess nuts boasting in an open foyer.*

———

One of rock and roll's earliest - and greatest - rock performers was the incomparable Buddy Holly. Despite his bespectacled, nerdy appearance, the man really knew how to ignite an audience. In fact, the folks who attended Buddy's performances got so excited that many of his concerts ended with a riot. Just as soon as the fans saw that Buddy had performed the closing song, they would fly into a collective rage, smash chairs, storm the stage, and tear down the curtain. So no theater owner would hire Buddy because they feared that their patrons would *wreck the halls, with bows of Holly.*

———————

A mother was pleased with the card her son had made her for Christmas, but was puzzled as to the scraggly-looking tree from which many presents dangled, and at the very top, something that looked strangely like a bullet. She asked him if he would explain the drawing and why the tree itself was so bare, instead of a fat pine tree. "It's not a traditional Christmas tree," he explained. "It's *a cartridge in a bare tree.*"

———————

Three circus midgets decided to change professions. They reviewed their options and decided to move to China and start a business together in that burgeoning economy. They bought a factory in Beijing and started manufacturing road-building materials to use to build highways for China's expanding transportation system. They shrewdly cornered the market on a black, sticky substance to cover the roads they were building. Thus, they became known as the *three wee kings of Orient tar.*

VIII
Name That Christmas Carol!

✤

When I was a callow youth, my neighborhood buddies and I used to sing a learned lyric that played around with levels of vocabulary:

Perambulate, perambulate, perambulate
your craft
Placidly down the liquid solution.
Ecstatically, ecstatically, ecstatically,
ecstatically:
Existence is but a delusion.

Translated into clear and simple English, our polysyllabic poem turned out to be *Row, row, row your boat.*

These days my youthful adventure in oblique obfuscation and polysyllabic poetry has evolved into a challenging game of sesquipedalian Christmas songs. Here are 35 pompously inflated titles of verses that you hear and perhaps sing during the month of December. Name each tune. Your task is to translate each ponderous version back into its original, nonorchidaceous form.

Example: Cup-Shaped Instruments Fashioned of a Whitish Metallic Element = "Silver Bells" The answers appear at the end of the chapter.

1. O Miniature Nazarene Village

2. Antlered Quadruped with the Cerise Proboscis

3. From Dark Till Dawn, Soundless and Sanctimonious

4. Locomote Hitherward, All You Steadfast

5. In a Distant Bovine Animal Feeding Station Improvised for a Child's Slumber

6. Pastoral Woollies Nocturnally Observed by Vigilant Herdsmen

7. My Sole Desire for the Yuletide Season is Receipt of Twin Anterior Incisors

8. Celestial Messengers From Splendid Empires

9. The Event Occurred at the Darkest Time With Visibility Unlimited

10. Ornament the Corridors with Sprigs of Berry-Bearing Evergreen

11. Exuberation to This Orb

12. Jehovah Bestow Upon You Rollicking Chevaliers Respite

13. The Fledgling Male Who Plays a Percussion Instrument

14. The Primordial Yuletide

15. Who is the Mystery Pre-adolescent?

33. I Shall Reappear at My Domicile for Yuletide

34. I Perceived a Trio of Nautical Vessels

35. The Diminutive Striped Squirrel Melody

Answers

1. O Little Town of Bethlehem 2. Rudolph the Red Nose Reindeer 3. Silent Night, Holy Night 4. Come All Ye Faithful 5. Away in a Manger

6. When Shepherds Watched Their Flocks By Night 7. All I Want for Christmas is My Two Front Teeth 8. Angels From the Realms of Glory 9. It Came Upon a Midnight Clear 10. Deck the Halls With Boughs of Holly

11. Joy to the World 12. God Rest Ye Merry, Gentlemen 13. The Little Drummer Boy 14. The First Noel 15. What Child Is This?

16. I Heard the Bells on Christmas Day 17. Christmastime is Near 18. I'm Dreaming of a White Christmas 19. Jingle Bells, Jingle Bells 20. I Saw Mommy Kissing Santa Claus

21. Do You Hear What I Hear? 22. Hark the Herald Angels Sing 23. We Three Kings of Orient Are 24. Here Comes Santa Claus 25. The Holly and the Ivy

26. Chestnuts Roasting on an Open Fire 27. Santa Claus Is Coming to Town 28. Let It Snow 29. The Twelve Days of Christmas 30. Frosty the Snowman

31. Walking Through a Winter Wonder land 32. Go Tell It on the Mountain 33. I'll Be Home for Christmas 34. I Saw Three Ships 35. The Chipmunk Song

Scoring

25-35
You have all the Yuletide spirit you need.

15-25
You could use something in your stocking.

0-14
Do you have the right holiday?

IX
. . . And a
Happy New Year

✼

More than two centuries ago, the most famous poet in Scotland was untimely ripped from this mortal coil. When Robert Burns died in 1796, he was but 37 years of age.

The life of Robert Burns might have furnished the plot for a romantic novel. He was born on January 25, 1759, in a clay cottage of two rooms in Alloway, near the southwestern coast of Scotland. His father was an unsuccessful farmer, and young Robert was assigned heavy work in the fields when he was only 11. The strain resulted in a progressive heart disease that was to prove fatal at the age of 37.

In 1786, Burns's life reached its low point. In despair over his poverty and the rejection by the woman he had hoped to marry, Burns resolved to emigrate from Scotland to Jamaica.

He gathered together some of his poems, hoping to sell them for a sum sufficient to pay the expenses of his journey. The result was a small volume of poetry titled *Poems, Chiefly in the Scottish Dialect*, and its impact changed the course of English verse.

Burns bought his ticket to Jamaica from the 20 pounds he earned from the sale of his little book. The night before he was to sail he wrote "Farewell to Scotland," which he intended to be his last song composed on Scottish soil. But in the morning he changed his mind, led partly by some dim foreshadowing of the result of his literary adventure.

In the late eighteenth century, with its emphasis on elegance, style and refined manners, the rustic, simple lyrics of Burns seemed incongruous. But *Poems, Chiefly in the Scottish Dialect* took all of Scotland by storm and was universally praised by critics. The newly famous author was dubbed The Peasant Poet and The Plowman Poet, and he became instantly lionized as a natural singer and rustic philosopher. Ultimately, Burns's work established him as the Scottish national poet and the primary bridge between the rational satire of the eighteenth century and the exuberant romanticism of the nineteenth.

Perhaps the most renowned of Burns's poems is "To a Mouse," subtitled "on turning her up in her nest with a plow, November 1785." Addressing the "wee beastie," the speaker apologizes for destroying the mouse's nest. Gradually, the parallels between man and mouse emerge:

> *But, Mousie, thou art no thy lane,*
> *In proving foresight may be vain;*
> *The best-laid schemes o' mice an' men*
>   *Gang aft a-gley,*
> *An lea'e us nought but grief an' pain*
>   *For promised joy.*

More than two centuries after Burns composed "To a Mouse," the power of its statement about the human condition struck a Nobel Prize winning American novelist. John Steinbeck crafted a simple and luminous story about two itinerant agricultural workers, Lenny and George, whose dreams of owning their own farm are crushed. He turned to Burns's statement "The best-laid schemes o' mice and men/Gang aft a-gley" (often go awry) and titled his novel *Of Mice and Men.*

Today, Robert Burns sings to us in another special way, for one of his lyrics is the first that many of us hear each year. On New Year's Eve, when the clock strikes midnight, the song that many bands around the world often play consists of verses written by Bobby Burns:

Should auld acquaintance be forgot,
    And never brought to min'?
Should auld acquaintance be forgot,
    And auld land syne?

For auld lang syne, my dear,
    For auld lang syne,
We'll take a cup o' kindness yet,
    For auld lang syne.

   In Scottish, "auld lang syne" (the last word should be sounded with a soft s, not a z) means literally "old long since," or "long ago," appropriate to the time when we review the joys and disappointments of the past year and hope for the best to come.
   Happy New Year.
   It's nice to have You Near

Or as others would say it:
    From Bugs Bunny:
    Hoppy New Year!

    From a puppy:
    Yappy New Year!

From a cat:
Happy Mew Year!

From a cow:
Happy Moo Year!

From a bull:
Happy New Steer!

From a water beast:
Hippo New Year!

From an expectant wildebeest:
Happy Gnu Year!

From a comedian:
Happy New Jeer!

From a priest:
Happy Pew Year!

From the poet Homer:
Harpy New Year!

From an aging flower child:
Hippie New Year, man!

From Puff Daddy:
Rappy New Year!

From a game-show host:
Happy Clue Year!

From a mechanic:
Happy New Gear!

From another mechanic:
Happy Lube Year!

From a jet pilot:
Happy New Lear!

From a cartographer:
Mappy New Year!

From a men's clothier:
Natty New Year!

From a job counselor:
Happy New Career!

From an attorney:
Happy Sued Year!

From a surfer:
Happy Dude Year!

From TV Guide:
Happy Viewed Year!

From Vincent Van Gogh:
Happy New Ear!